Archer Addy

True Stories 'cause I'm telling them

I'm Trying Something New

Erik Nachtrieb with Tracy Nachtrieb
Illustrated by Hayden Beaty
Edited by Jenny Kanevsky

Published by 1iOpen Productions, LLC
Seattle, Washington U.S.A.

ISBN: 978-0-692-28825-2

DEDICATION

Dedicated to our daughter, Addison Nachtrieb, and all of the young people, girls and boys, who ask more of themselves than is expected. And, to those at The Nock Point and Next Step Archery.

CONTENTS

ACKNOWLEDGMENTS

We would like to acknowledge the greater archery community. Thank you for contributing to Addy's success and supporting us in development and writing this of this book. It was a daunting task to help a young girl excel in a sport about which we knew nothing and then quite bold for us to put that experience into a book. Thank you all for embracing us. This is a book about archery, but more than that, it is a book about determination in youth; we hope to foster in others.

We would also like to acknowledge those who provided financial support for this endeavor; family, friends and strangers, all brought together to help us take the first step in this book series.

Thank you Ron/Grandpa for introducing a young girl to her passion, to Coach Rob for answering our incessant questions, to Addy's Bow Mechanic Brian for teaching me how a bow works, to Hayden for revising the illustrations. Over and over again, to Jenny for making us sound like writers, and to our family for waiting patiently for us to finish this book.

A special thanks to Addy's sister, Riley, who is often overshadowed by her younger sister's success, attention and popularity due to archery. You have been a very understanding and supportive sister and daughter. Thank you.

Archer Addy

Bow String

Cams

Limbs

Arrow Rest

Sight

Draw Arm

Release

Nock

Fletch

Arrows

Quiver Candy

Quiver

Arrow Counter

Scope

Arrow Tip

Riser

Cables

Arm Guard

Compound Bow

On the line

I shift my feet at the line, settling into my stance on the hardwood floor. I hear nothing. I see nothing. It's me, my arrow and the target. That's all there is. Moving my eyes from the target to my quiver, I choose an arrow. I'm in slow motion. I gently lower the arrow to rest on my bow.

Click.

The arrow nocks onto my bow string. It's the only sound I hear besides my breath.

My trigger locks in. I raise my bow to the target, narrow my eyes. My grip softens as I draw back my string. Silence. My muscles load.

My bow has power. My draw comes to anchor off the tip of my nose, the corner of my mouth. My focus moves through to my distant target. I can feel the arrow's strike point.

My breathing slows and my bow settles down on the target center. As my eyes drift to the X my back muscles contract increasing trigger tension. NOW! The trigger releases the string, my bow expands, my arrow leaps from the string and the bow falls forward! Everything explodes with speed and power.

I remain still, silent. Everything moves in slow motion. I watch as my beautiful arrow, carbon fiber and aluminum, smooth and black with pink fletching, flexes in midair and fights to maintain its flight path. I don't take my eyes off her. She wants to find the X, the spider. My eyes follow her to the target. THWAK! She kills the spider, the target X! I knew she would. That's what we train for.

I'm Addy. I'm nine years old. I'm just a girl . . . an archer girl.

Chapter 1: You're Not Ready

"I want to win a medal, Dad."

I really do. All my friends have trophies in soccer, baseball, and all kinds of sports. My friend Casey even has a bunch of trophies in Jujitsu. I don't even know what that is. Some kind of wrestling or something. But, he gets a lot of trophies. "You're not ready, Addy." "But Dad, I practice all the time." Dad said the only tournament coming up was the big one. The Nationals.

"I don't care. I just want to shoot my bow and win a medal."

"Addy, people train for at least a year to go to The Nationals."

The Indoor National Archery tournament is like the biggest tournament ever. Everyone in the whole country competes. The one with the highest score wins the National Championship! I think when you get older you get afraid to do things. I'm not afraid. Everyone is worried I will feel bad if I don't win. A medal would be nice, but I don't care just about that. How will I ever know how good I am if I don't try against the best? How come that doesn't make sense to adults?

I give Dad a grumpy look and plop down on my bed.

"I've practiced for four months. I can do it Dad." I look up with a wrinkled forehead. This works on Dad sometimes.

There's no way Dad falls for that sad, mopey face stuff, crying, or being a brat. Using that stuff is like trying to get your sister to help clean your room. It just doesn't work, ever.

It took me awhile to figure out what works on Dad. He always says, "Determination" or "Tough it out," "Soldier on," and "Suck it up." These are the things he likes. So when I want something, I don't whine about it. I stand tall, look him in the eye the best I can—he's really tall— wrinkle my forehead and give him my best, *I'm determined to get what I want and nothing is going to stop me*, look.

He narrows his eyes back at me and we come to an understanding. Works every time!

"Let me think about it."

Darn! This eventually means no. Parents are afraid to say "No." When they don't want to say "Yes" they always say, "Let me think about it." They think they're being sneaky, but kids know they're just coming up with a reason to say no. And, their reasons are never any good. That's why they take forever to explain them. So, we get confused and bored. And, they never actually say "No" either. They talk and talk, blah blah blah, making no sense. They wonder why we keep asking and bugging them. It's because they never actually just say "No." Duh!

So, anyway, I don't know if I'm going to the National Tournament or not. I'm in Dad's "let me think about it" place. Probably means no, but I can keep asking. Every day.

Chapter 2: Thinking About It

The next day I have back yard practice.

It is so cold, I can see my breath in the air. The grass crunches, it's frozen under my feet! We live in the coldest place in the whole world. Almost next to Alaska, but still where the sun comes up. I have to practice in the cold a lot because our winter is five months long. Dad says it makes me a tougher archer. I think it just makes me cold. A lot.

Today, I'm training for the Nationals, even though Dad is trying to figure out how to tell me I can't go. I want to show him I'm ready. I shoot my arrows from sixty feet. I know because I helped Dad measure the target distance. At first, it seemed so far, but I practice a lot and it gets closer. I'm shooting one hundred arrows today.

I know Dad is going to check on me. He

pretends he is just standing there, raking leaves, cutting branches, inspecting the yard like it might change right in front of his face, but he is watching me shoot. I know it.

"Nice shooting Addy."

I just put three arrows in the target. I look back at him and smile. I shoot three more and look back at him with a smug look. *See Dad, I'm ready.* I hope he can read my mind.

Dad smiles and goes back in the house. Maybe my shooting is helping him to "think about it."

I wait days to find out how long Mom and Dad were going to "think about it." Days for adults seem like only a couple of hours. They don't get it. For kids, days are like weeks and months of waiting. It's all we think about. The one thing we want. I want to go to The National Tournament.

Finally, after what seems like months, Mom and Dad ask to talk with me.

"Have a seat on the couch, Addy."

This is how saying "No" always starts with Dad. Last time Mom and Dad sat me and my sister down on the couch, they told us Dad was going to go to Africa for like a month. I didn't cry, because we aren't supposed to cry. But, I was sad for a real long time.

I'm sad now. My eyes start getting wet, but I don't let them see. I try to sit up straight on the lumpy couch. I really don't want them to say "No." I practiced so much. I hold the edge of the couch and wrinkle my forehead.

Mom sits next to Dad on the ottoman. Dad smiles at me. Oh, great. I slump. He is going to try and make saying "No" a positive thing.

"OK, Addy," he says "We'll enter you into the tournament!"

What!? I swallow real big and stare at them. They stare at me. OMG!

I jump at my Dad and hug him as hard as I can. Awesome! I'm going! I don't even know what to say I just keep hugging him and looking at Mom.

Dad pushes me back, holds me in his hands and looks in my eyes.

"But it's going to be a challenge for you."

I want to burst out of his grip and run around the living room waving my arms.

"I know. I know. Thank you Daddy!"

His head comes back to look at me closer.

"Here's the deal."

Oh, here we go again with Dad's deals. Who cares? I'm going to the tournament. Yeah!

"OK?"

"If you start this, you have to finish it. If you are doing well or you are doing poorly, you have to shoot the whole tournament. Both days."

"Yeah. Yeah. Yeah. I will. I will."

"Do you understand?"

"Yes. Yes. I'm so excited!"

Maybe couch talks aren't always so bad.

Chapter 3: Better Than Boys

My Grandpa likes shooting a bow and arrow. He'd always tried to get my mom to do it. I asked her why she didn't want to shoot the bow.

"Hmmm . . . I don't know," she once told me. "It was kind of a sport for boys when I was a little girl."

Yeah, I can do what boys can do.

Last summer, Grandpa had a new bow for each of the cousins. The bow was small and looked really complicated. It had lots of strings and wheels and other stuff all over it. It was made of some kind of metal and painted black and camouflage. Pretty much the most popular boy colors ever.

I never saw an Indian in the movies or in a book with a bow and arrow like this. I bet no one could shoot this thing.

"This is a compound bow." Grandpa said.

He was holding it up and telling us all kinds of things about it. My cousins and I looked at each other. They definitely didn't know what he was saying either. Grandpa seemed really proud.

He said you put an arrow on the string.

"This is nocking the arrow."

Then he pulled back the string and the arrow looked like it was going to fly off.

"This is drawing the arrow. Then you aim using the sight."

The sight looked like the glass end of a ship captain's telescope.

"Look at the sight and the target at the same time."

At the same time? How can you look at two things at the same time? I scrunched up my face, focused, and crossed my eyes. Everything was blurry and double.

"This is not a toy!" he boomed.

It sure looked like a toy in his big giant hands.

"Do you hunt with it Grandpa?" I wanted to know.

"No. It's too small. It's for fun shooting." Seems like a toy to me. Maybe he is too old to remember what a toy is. Grandpa kept telling us all the rules.

"Ask to use it. Always have an adult around. Only shoot the target . . . " And on, and on, don't point it at the dog. Don't shoot your sister. Don't take it apart. Put it away when you're done. It was definitely a toy.

This was getting boring. I was standing there in the burning sun in the rocky driveway, my shoulders felt too heavy to even hold it up. Grandpas have been doing this talking thing a lot longer than parents. He can talk three times as long as Dad. Couldn't we just do it?

"Who wants to try it first?"

Of course my cousin Jackson wanted to. Boys are always thinking they are the best at everything because they're boys. Grandpa is a boy too and he got a big smile when Jackson raised his hand. Grandpas always want to teach the boys.

"OK, Jackson. Hold it like this. Nock the arrow on the string. Hold it up. Pull the string back. Aim at the target. Shoot!"

There was no way Jackson was going to see anything with his hair in his face like that. He thinks it's so cool. Boys wear their hair like that now. I call it backwards hair.

Jackson flipped his hair back for the hundredth time so he could see. I wonder if his eyes are crossed, or even open!?

Twang! And the arrow didn't even hit the target. It bounced off a tree and into the bushes. Boys! I smiled.

"Addy. Do you want to try it?" Me? Dang Grandpa saw me.

Chapter 4: The Natural

I'd rather go back on the iPad, I thought. I had

downloaded a new app and wanted to play before Mom made me go out and listen to Grandpa tell us about this toy that is not a toy.

"OK. I guess." Let's get this over with.

I think Grandpa made all this up. I'm standing here with one of Grandma's cut off socks on my arm, it's supposed to protect me from the string. I have a rope tied around my waist with a tube hanging down. It was holding the arrows and I bet he totally made it in his workshop.

Grandpas make everything in their workshops. He even made Mom a Christmas present in his workshop once. She really liked it when she opened it. But, I never saw it again when we got home.

I also had a big camouflage glove on my hand to pull back the string and of course the toy bow. OMG! There was Dad taking like a million pictures of me. This wasn't even cute and none of it was pink, which of course I love and is my favorite color. You should always wear something pink. There was nothing pink about Grandpa's archery. I just looked totally dorky.

If my friends at school saw me, I couldn't even pull this off as a new fashion statement. So, of course, Dad would take pictures.

"Alright Addy, keep a light grip on the bow. Nock your arrow. Pull back the string to the corner of your mouth. Hold it, aim and let go of the string when you're ready."

This seemed pretty easy. I squinted to see the bow's red dot. I had to line it up with the target. I tried to look at them both at the same time, the red dot and the target. So far I wasn't cross-eyed.

The red dot kept moving. It didn't seem so easy now. I tried to hold my arms still. I took a slow breath like Grandpa said. . . .

THWAK! I opened my eyes. This wasn't a toy!

"Wow, Addy!"

Dad was running up taking all kinds of pictures of the target.

I looked at Jackson. I must have done pretty well because he flipped his hair and just looked around like it was no big deal and he was bored of watching. *Yeah, just keep looking away. It won't change that I hit the target and you didn't.*

I just stood there smiling while Dad, Grandpa and my sister were like a bunch of squirrels around the target. I couldn't see anything. But, I knew.

"Addy! You're a natural!" Grandpa yelled back from the target. I'm not sure what that meant, but when I finally saw my arrow had hit the X on the target, all I knew was, if there was more pink in archery, I just might shoot some more.

Chapter 5: Here's The Deal

Once a year, in the summer, we visit Grandpa's house in Idaho. It's hot. I mean really hot. Like, hot enough to catch snakes when they come out to warm up. I always catch baby snakes there. I kept one for a pet once, but, in about a month, it died of old age. Mom said I probably helped it get old fast.

Grandpa's house is in the woods with an old people's yard. It has all kinds of strange balls of glass, fake deer and little people made of cement, fake birds, benches and stuff. Grandma says it's art for the yard. I think it looks like they stole a bunch of stuff from Disneyland.

Real deer and moose come into yard at night. I like to watch them. I hang over the back of the couch looking out the huge picture window. It's as tall as the house and as wide as the room. But, if I was a deer, I wouldn't go in a yard with art that looked like me.

At Grandpa's that visit, I kept shooting. I shot on the side of Grandpa's shop near the woods. We were there like a week and I was the only one who wanted to shoot. I think it was because I could hit the target and nobody else could. Grandpa was helping me a lot, even though I'm a girl. I was shooting awesome and it was easy to forget all about my iPad. The bow was lite in my hand. It made me feel strong. I have seagull eyes. Not eagle eyes. Everyone always corrects me, but really I have seagull eyes. That's what people with good eyes have in Seattle. We have lots of seagulls.

My eyes helped me shoot strait. I shot every day until we left. When I shot it I felt like I could do it for the rest of my life.

On the last day, the adults all came out to watch me shoot one last time before we had to go home. Everybody was smiling down at me real strange, like they found something super special they had been looking for. I remember thinking: I can make this work for me.

"Grandpa, can I have the bow?" Their smiles turned strange. Dad looked at Grandpa and raised his eyebrows.

"Well, I don't know Addy. This is for all of the cousins to use when they visit."

I looked around. My sister was in the house on the iPad. Jackson was on the patio with his PlayStation. The other kids were playing with the dog.

Yeah, right. No one else even shot the bow the whole week. Grownups are always trying to be fair. Even when it doesn't make any sense and the kids don't care. They were probably trying to teach me some kind of lesson. They're always full of lessons. They can never just say "Yes."

"Pleeeease!?!"

Dad and Grandpa started talking. I couldn't hear but their eyebrows were scrunched up and they sounded serious. I don't think this is going to go well.

Both their heads turned back to me. I looked at them, Mom looked at them. Uh oh!

"How much do you like shooting the bow?" Dad's eyes narrowed. He was trying to look inside my head for the answer.

Huh? I just asked if I could have it. Duh. Why do adults always ask dumb questions?

"I like it . . . a lot?"

"But, do you like it enough to keep shooting?"

"Uh, yeah."

"Will you keep shooting or just take it home and not use it?"

Why do adults ask the same dumb questions over and over again? It's the same question and same answer, but they want to hear the answer a bunch of times. Oh. My. Gosh. I like the bow. I want the bow. I asked for the bow. Nobody else wants it. Can I have it already?

"I will shoot it all the time, Dad."

"OK, Addy. Here's the deal."

There it is. I just got in over my head. When Dad starts a sentence with "a deal" it always means I have to do a bunch of stuff.

Dad is like a free app. You totally download a cool game on Mom's iPhone. It's free. You're doing super awesome in the game, make the next level, and there it is. Ads start blocking your game and you can't get any special powers without money. Dad was about to make me pay for my new special powers.

"Grandpa and I have decided . . ." Oh man! ". . . if you really enjoy shooting and want the bow . . ." I like said that ten times, ". . . then you need to make an agreement with Grandpa. You have to practice shooting every other day for three months. If you do this for three months you can keep the bow. If you miss more than a few days, you have to give it back. Does that make sense? Can you do that?"

"Yes!" Oh wait! Every other day! What if it rains? What if it's cold?

"That's rain or shine and even if it's cold. When Grandpa shoots his bow it doesn't matter what the weather is."

I hate it when they read your mind. Sometimes I try not to think things because I know they can figure out what I'm thinking. I forgot this time.

"OK."

"Are you sure?"

"Yes."

"Even if there is snow on the ground?" Here we go again with the questions.

"Yes, Dad."

I was so excited to show my friends my new bow. OK. I knew it wasn't a toy. I was told that like a billion times. But it was still cool! It was shiny black with camo and would look awesome once I put some pink feathers on my arrows and got rid of the sock. This is a super girl's bow! I was going to shoot all the time!

My friends would come watch me. I'd be the best in the whole world! I was going to be an archer!

Chapter 6: I Do Everything Myself

We have been home a day. It's time to shoot so I can keep the bow. The target is in the garage and I have to lean all the way over to drag it out by a rope. I always hear Dad say, "Put your back into it." I did, but that doesn't make it easier. When you're a kid you ask a lot of questions you already know the answer to. If I asked for help the answer would be: "You have to learn to do things yourself, Addy."

Myself? I can do lots of things myself. I can log onto Netflix. I can ride my bike and a unicycle. I can change Mom's iPhone wallpaper.

I take care of my hermit crab and I know where my sister keeps her phone and I know her laptop's password.

I think what he means is I have to do really heavy hard stuff myself. Stuff regular parents would help me with.

"Dad, it's heavy! I can't do it."

"Should we bring the bow back?" Ugh!

Of course, Grandpa gave me the hugest target ever: A giant block of foam wider than my arms and as tall as me. I might have to jump off it later.

Even though I only have to hit a tiny little X, he said it was so big because I need a lot of space for the arrows that miss the X. Looks like he still thinks I will shoot like a girl. I'll show him how girls shoot.

I get the target set up in the yard. I use

Dad's tape measure to figure out where to shoot. He said to make it at ten yards. I don't know how much that is and have to do math to figure out how many feet make up ten yards. It's not hard. I do multiplication. It's about as far as you can throw a rock and still make it worth throwing. I use my sister's iPhone to make the feet into yards. I know the password on that too. Don't tell her.

The target is all set up. I tie the rope around my waist with the arrow tube and put Grandma's totally unfashionable sock on my arm. I'm going to have to change that real soon. I don't think cool archers wear a sock. I pick up my bow and start to nock an arrow.

"That's right Addy. Now, make sure you draw the string back to your anchor at the corner of your mouth. Keep your grip light. Keep your bow arm strong. Focus."

Oh, now he wants to help. Dad always says to do things yourself, he won't help you, and then when you start doing them he starts telling you how to do them. All of a sudden he's helping you so much you're not sure if you're doing anything yourself.

"I know Dad. I got it Dad. Dad! I can't focus!"

"Oh. Yes, focus." Dad takes a step back.

Thwak! Cool. Thwak! Yes. Thwak! Awesome! I totally hit the target! Hmmm, I'm going to have to figure out how to hit the X.

Chapter 7: My Audience

I practice every other day for the rest of the summer.

I still have a month to go in my "deal." It's Fall and getting cold. I look out the window and don't want to go out and shoot. Dad is out there and I can see his breath. All the leaves are on the ground waiting to be raked. No more flowers or birds. Just a lot of sticks pretending to be bushes, and my target staring at me, wondering if I am going to come out and shoot.

Oh dang! Dad sees me in the window and waves. I can tell he is reading my mind again. He smiles and points to the target.

I need a plan.

"Mom! Can you make some hot chocolate! I have to go shoot and it's super cold out. Dad is going to make me freeze to death!"

Mom is awesome. She's not like a real Mom. She is real pretty and always dresses cool. I think I got my fashion sense from her. It definitely wasn't from Dad. He wears stuff just because it functions, whatever that means. Mom wears lots of stuff because it looks good, like me. And, she makes the best hot chocolate! It's warm on your lips, but not too hot because she adds a little cold water. Plus, she puts layers of mini-marshmallows on top until it overflows. Yum! I pick them off with my fingers first!

Now I'm ready. I have my super cool pink stocking hat on with a ponytail hole, my puffy pink coat with three shirts and my favorite skinny jeans. The jeans are cold, but they look cool, which makes being cold OK.

It is really cold. My new bow is metal and holding it is like holding an icicle.

"Dad, this is super cold. I can't hold it."

Dad is like a Grandpa in training. He doesn't have a workshop but he can make all kinds of things from whatever. He goes in the house and gets some old knit gloves. Just like that, he cuts some fingers out of them—just a few so I can shoot the bow but still hold it. Dads never pay attention to the little things. The gloves don't even match! I don't complain though. My hands are warm. I'm guessing Mom would complain; I think one of the gloves is from one of her favorite pairs.

I'm really going to have to change this outfit. Yes, more pink and there has to be something better than a rope and tube to carry my arrows. I'm going to have to get a job. Mom says if you want lots of stuff you have to work for it. I think I will make my own job and pay myself lots of money.

I can see my breath. My bow is cold and I have like a million clothes on. I wonder if Mom made the hot chocolate yet. Dad thinks he's being sneaky. I see him. He's peaking around the fence, watching me. I'm just standing here . . . freezing! Parents test you all the time. Dad wants to see if I'm going to actually shoot. He probably thinks I'm going to ask to go inside. I pretend I don't see him. I raise my bow and nock an arrow. I see his eyes widen. I lower my bow. His eyes narrow. I try not to smile. I start to raise it again. I put it down. Ha ha!

I'll show him. I raise my bow. He better watch now. Thwak! He smiles and walks back behind the fence. That's it, a little smile?! I totally hit it in the blue! OK, well it's not in the yellow but I hit it. Now I don't have anyone watching. What if I hit an X? I'll be the only one to see it. I wish I was in a giant stadium and everyone could see me.

Great. Now, it's raining. Ump. Here comes my audience of one. Dad and an umbrella.

"Hey, Addy, I brought an umbrella out for you. It's great you're shooting. I wouldn't want you to have to stop because of the rain." Of course he wouldn't.

It's freezing and raining. Normal people would go inside and have hot chocolate. But not parents, they always figure out a way for you to keep doing anything, no matter how miserable you are. They're not helping as much as they think. If Dad really wanted to help he would bring me my marshmallowy hot chocolate.

"Thanks, Dad."

And there it is, the school bus coming down my street! I walk home; we live really close to school. But, lots of my friends take the bus. This is my chance! They will all see me. They will believe that I'm an archer girl. I'll be a star at school! I'll walk through the playground, kids asking me questions about archery. Even boys! They'll take lots of pictures. I'll be on Facebook with like a hundred likes, shared all over Instagram. . . .But, Dad has the umbrella over me. No one is going to see me!

"Dad, you don't have to hold the umbrella. It's OK."

"Addy, it's raining."

"I know. But, I have to learn to shoot in the rain, right?"

"Are you sure?"

Doesn't he get it? I'm about to be a star. Come on Dad, hurry up and move the umbrella or none of my friends will see me! The bus is getting closer.

It's slowing down! I raise my bow to aim at the target. The bus stops. I look out of the corner of my eye. It's stopped! A bunch of my friends' faces are smashed against the rainy windows steaming them up. So cool! I draw back and thwak!

This is the best day ever. Be cool. I lower my bow and wave at my friends. I can hear them yelling through the windows, "Addy! Addy! What is that? What are you doing? Is that yours?"

Yep, it's mine. I hold my bow proudly.
This is my bow and I'm an archer. An archer
girl!

Chapter 8: All Mine

The target I put above my bed is so cool. Every time I look up, I think about shooting it. It makes me think about archery more. If you are going to be good at something you have to think about it a lot. After High School, adults go to even more school, just to think about something for a long time. Even for years. Lying on my bed, I think, if I am going to be the best in the world, I have to get better. I'm pretty sure Dad has given me all the advice he has about archery and I can only talk to Grandpa on the phone.

Mom and Dad always say, if you want to know something, look it up yourself first. Since my sister is at her friend's and I know her laptop password, I decide to look things up there.

"Addy, did you ask your sister if you could be on her computer?"

I think Mom already knew the answer. This is where she wants to hear it from me. If I answer her real fast sometimes it works.

"No. But, I don't have one and I need to learn archery and I found some videos on YouTube that teach me how to be better and I want to be better and Dad doesn't know archery and I don't know who to ask." I take a breath.

Mom just stands there. If I do this right, it will seem like I said a lot of stuff and she will be too busy to say "No."

"OK. But, ask next time."

Yep, works every time. If you do something you're not supposed to, make sure you're learning something while you're doing it.

So, I find all kinds of stuff on YouTube, and none of it looks like what I'm doing. I watch people who do archery for a job, the Olympics, and people in their back yards. They have really cool bars on their bows. Their bows are all kinds of cool colors. They have sights with all kinds of dials and measurers. All kinds of stuff is attached to their bows. They don't even use their fingers. They pull back their string with a cool looking metal thing. Awesome!

I watch lots of girl archers shooting in videos. I have to go try what they were doing. I grab my hat, jacket, my boots go on, gloves on and there's my cold bow, I go into the backyard to copy them right away before I forget what I saw. I imagine I'm in the Olympics. I'm glad they let girls in the Olympics. I would have a pink bow. I wonder if they even make pink bows.

I need to find out if other girls in my city shoot bows. We could make an archery club and all shoot together and listen to music. I'll teach some of my friends how to shoot too.

"Addy, guess what!"
Dad shouts from the back porch to the frozen backyard where I'm shooting.

"What, Dad?"

"Grandpa called and wanted to congratulate you on getting to keep the bow."

I forgot all about it. I didn't even remember I shot every other day for three months. It didn't seem like it. I was having fun.

"Awesome! I really get to keep it?"

"It's all yours."

This is the best! I am an archer with my own bow. I am so excited. I finished up shooting and run inside with my bow. I clear off the top of my dresser and lay out my bow and arrows on it, with my rope and tube. I sit back on my bed and stare at my bow. It's mine. I will take really good care of it. Maybe I will paint it pink.

Now, how to get to the Olympics. . . .

Chapter 9: Fashionable Rules

So, that's how I got my start in archery and now I'm entered in my first Archery Tournament ever. I have to figure out how it works. Mom and Dad can't help me. No one in my family can even help me. I am the only archer.

The USA Indoor National Archery Championship Rules, Equipment and Conduct manual has 119 pages. OMG, 119 pages! Adults make so many rules and you have to read them all. You can't even watch them on TV. If we could watch all the reading stuff on TV, I think we would all be good readers.

I print out all 119 pages on Dad's computer. He lets me use it if I ask. I run out of paper two times.

Yep, my first tournament! The National Championships! I'll be going against everyone in my country. I don't know how many people that is. In school they say there are like a billion people ever, but they don't all do archery. So, I think it will be like a million people. But, I only go against the girls.

Wow, this is a lot of reading. There are rules on how to score; rules on how to stand; rules on what to wear. I read lots of rules on my bed. But I pay good attention on what to wear. That has to be the most important. I have to look fashionable.

I try on tights and skirts, shirts and shoes. My whole closet is on the floor. Mom walks in. She doesn't look too happy.

"I hope you're going to pick all this up when you're done. What are you doing?"

I twirl around to show Mom. I choose a tan skirt over my black tights. The rules say my skirt has to be as long as my fingers against my side. I'm wearing a long sleeve purple shirt and my black tennis shoes.

"I'm getting my archery outfit ready!" I give her a big smile. I think I have a great outfit. It even matches and that's super important. Mom says I am really good at matching and fashion. She says I match up the most unique clothes she would never think of. I like being unique.

Dad comes up behind Mom in the doorway of my room.

"Addy. This is a serious tournament. It's about how much you practiced and your focus. Not what you wear."

I flick my hair back and look up at Dad.

"I shoot better if I look good." I give him an even bigger smile.

Dad just stares at me with squinted eyes and grins. He doesn't know what to say. I know. He always wants me to shoot better. I can usually do whatever I want if it helps me shoot better.

But it's true! Every girl knows it. You do lots of things better if you match. I like to have cool matching clothes and when I do, I can do anything. Boys just don't get it.

"Well, you look great Addy. I think you will shoot great." See, Mom gets it. I wasn't done though.

"Mom, I want to paint my nails for the tournament."

"Really? What color?"

"All the colors of my target! Can I use your colors?"

Mom and I walk to the bathroom and she starts pulling out her nail polish.

"Are you going to paint them yourself?"

"Yep, I can do it. I want, black, blue, red, and yellow."

I go jump onto my bed with my target and Mom brings in the colors. Dad peeks in on me.

"Painting your nails the same colors as the target?"

"Yep!" I hold up one partially finished set of colorful fingers.

"My thumb and pinky are blue like the five and six ring. The next two fingers red like the seven and eight ring. And, most important: the center finger is yellow for the nine ring, ten ring and the spider!"

"I thought when you shoot you are supposed to 'be the arrow,' not the target?"

"Dad!" Sheesh, he doesn't know anything.

"I'm focused on the target, Dad. That's all I think about."

He rolls his eyes. He just doesn't understand fashion and archery.

I finish painting my nails and they look awesome with bright yellow on my middle finger surrounded by all the other colors. I feel like I can do anything.

I lay in bed the night before Nationals staring up at the target I had taped above my bed. I focus on the yellow center. I imagine all my arrows going into the yellow. I think if I pretend it enough it will happen when I really shoot. I close my eyes and try to pretend really hard.

Chapter 10: Tournament Day

I think I fell asleep because when I open my eyes it's Mom telling me it's time to get dressed for the tournament.

"Time to get up sweetie, it's tournament day!"

Not a problem. I have the best outfit ever. I stretch in bed and then get up. I smell eggs cooking. My favorite, sunny side up eggs. I like to see the bright yolk. It makes me happy and tastes good too. And it's yellow in the center, like my target. I always ask for sunny side up. That means it's really runny on top. I poke a hole in the yolk and eat that first. It's the best way to eat an egg.

On tournament day you have to eat a good breakfast. I ask Mom to cut up an apple and if I can also have a yogurt.

"Are you nervous honey?" Mom put my eggs on the table.
I hopped up onto the breakfast stool.

"Nope. I'm not at the tournament yet. I don't think I'll be nervous. I can't wait to shoot!" Dad sits down next to me with his always serious look.

"Addy, I know you are very excited. I think you are going to do very well, but remember your scoring is going to be compared to every other girl shooting a bow who is between nine and twelve years old, and you are nine. So don't get your hopes up. I don't want you to be disappointed. Just do your best."

"I'll do my best Dad. But, I think I will do really good." I don't look up and eat more of my eggs. Yummy.

I think Dad is really worried about the tournament. It just doesn't bother me. I just want to shoot. After breakfast, I see Dad in my room looking at my bow, checking my arrows and making sure I have enough food and water. He sees me walk by the door.

"Come here, Addy."

I go and sit on my bed. I'm not sure if I should smile. I just look at him.

"I'm real proud of you Addy. Are you ready?"

I smile. "I'm ready Dad. Don't worry I'll be OK." I think I make Dad happy. He smiles and winks at me.

"OK, girl. I'll be right there if you need me. Let's go."

He pats me on the back and walks away,
leaving me there, alone, just me and my bow.

Chapter 11: I'm Not a Lady!

Today is the day! The 44th U.S. Indoor National Archery Tournament. That's what the banner says, way up high on the building when I get out of the car. Oh man! I'm here!

"Riley, off the ipad and out of the car!" I think Dad says this 100 times a day to my sister. She's not to excited about watching archery all day. I like that she's here.

"Come on Riley. Let's go." I tell her. I want to get to the tournament and she's slowly sliding out of the car, half putting the iPad away half looking at it. She just ignores everyone. I know she's listening. She's real smart and hears everything. But, when you get 11 you have to be cool. I understand. I'm going to be cool like her someday.

My whole family is here! Dad and I carry the archery gear ahead of Mom with a grocery bag full of all of my favorite stuff. Riley slowly keeps up with us just enough to be with us, but far enough behind so she can pretend she might be by herself.

Yesterday mom took me to the grocery store. She said I could get anything I wanted to eat at the tournament. Eating good is the most important thing to my mom. So when she says I can get anything I want, she means like carrots, water, and healthy stuff.

"Can I get a pop and potato chips?" I always try. Sometimes you can wear parents down. Not mom.

"Only good food Addy. Look here are some veggie chips. There just like potato chips."

Really mom! We end up with water, veggie chips, sliced apple, string cheese, cut carrots, and my total all-time favorite snack, dried seaweed. Really, it's awesome!

Dad and I head to check-in "What's your name?" The lady at the desk asks me. She doesn't smile.

"Addy," I whisper. Being at the tournament doesn't make me nervous but all the adults do.

"Female Bowman Compound Freestyle?" she asks. She wants to know what category I'm in. I know the answer but look up at Dad anyway. Sometimes looking at Dad makes things better. He nods to me that it's correct.

"Yes," I say. The no smiling lady looks at me again.

"Go get your equipment checked for safety." She points her pen into the next room full of people and bows.

I look up at Dad again. He nods at me and toward the equipment check. Dad walks in front of me but at the door he steps aside to let me go first. I stop.

At the other side of the room an old guy looks at me. I look down and then back up. He is still looking at me.

Can't he just look away? Old people just stare at you all the time. Like Grandparents, but not as bad. Grandparents stare at you and then hug you and kiss you and don't let you go.

I hear Dad behind me. "Addy, this is your tournament. You have to do things yourself."

This is one of the things about archery. In archery, you have to do things yourself. The adults help you but they don't do anything for you. It's not like real life where your parents wake you up, make you breakfast, drive you where you want to go, carry your stuff.

In archery they always say, "We're not teaching you archery. We're teaching you about life." I don't get it. I never see anyone walking around in real life, with a bow and arrow. What does shooting a target have to do with teaching me about life?

Riley's eleven, she teaches me about life all the time and we never use a bow and arrow. The other day she showed me her books on growing up and how babies are made and stuff.

Maybe I'm not a good enough archer for them to teach me about growing up yet.

The old guy is still staring at me. Ugh! Then he smiles and waves me over to him. Dad bumps me forward. I start walking. At least Dad was right behind me. That made me feel good.

"What's your name young lady?"

Lady?! I saw Riley's growing up books. I'm not a lady. They are old and wear all kinds of funny stuff under their clothes.

"I'm Addy and I'm a girl archer." I grin up at him.

The old guy's head pulls back and looks at me funny. I keep staring at him. Yep, that's right, I'm a girl archer.

"Well, girl archer Addy. Can I look at your bow?"

I raise my bow up to him proudly. I cleaned it the night before and it's all shiny. It's an awesome bow. The one my Grandpa got. It's not pink, but my parents said if I stick with archery and practice for a year I might get a new bow. And it can be any color I want. It will be pink of course!

"This is a cute little bow Addy. It looks like a toy bow."

"It is not a toy!" I look at him sternly. "I shoot a lot of arrows with it."

"Oh, I was just kidding. You're right, bows aren't toys. It's just so small."

"I'm small. I'm nine. But I can shoot it real good."

I don't care if I win this tournament or not. I'm going to show them how good my bow is and how good I can shoot it. Everyone always wants to see my bow, to see if it is real. I'll show them how real it is.

"Well it looks like your, 'not a toy bow,' is in good condition and meets all of the rules. Good luck young . . . girl." He smiles big and gives my bow back.

Now what? I stand there with my bow, the old guy still smiling at me with all his big crazy teeth. I look up at Dad. He just shrugs his shoulders. I don't know what to do. I can't just stand here. There are people in line behind me. I looked back up at the old guy.

"You need to get your scorecard and lane assignment."

He says, pointing to the next room. I turn and start walking, leaving Dad behind. Oh man, that was almost embarrassing. I can't look like I don't know what I'm doing. I told Dad I could do this. Dad catches up to me when the lady is giving me my score cards.

"There are two score cards," she says. "You have to score on both with your shooting partners."

Shooting partners? I didn't read about this. Uh oh! Who will they be? What they will look like? What if it's a boy or an adult?

"Once you're done scoring you have to double check your score. Then you all have to sign each other's score cards. Then you turn them into the judge."

Wow. That's a lot of stuff to remember. There is a whole lot more to this than I thought. I scrunch up my forehead to try and remember what she was saying. I hope Dad is listening.

"Do you understand all of that, young lady?"

Girl. I'm a girl!

I nod my scrunched up forehead, take my score cards and start walking to the tournament range. It's almost time; I know because Dad keeps reminding me the time.

"Ten minutes until you start, Addy."

"I know, Dad."

I can read a clock, too. But parents always seem to want to tell you how much time you have. And, tell you every minute.

"Five minutes." Ugh!

"I know Dad."

I think he's getting nervous. I look up and he is looking around everywhere, at everything.

I grab his hand and hold it. We walk towards the Tournament Range together.

Chapter 12: I'm Here

Dad and I walk down a long hallway.

Archers are walking back and forth from the range to the check-in rooms. Kid archers, adult archers, boys, girls, men, every kind of person is there. Holding onto Dad's hand I have to dodge bows and people to not get bumped. The walls are covered with plaques, trophies, and pictures of important archers, all of them looking down on me, wondering what I'm doing there.

It's getting louder the closer we get. I hear people talking, moving bows around, the timing clock beeping. Everyone is talking over each other. They're all talking too much, just like

Dad. I think people like to talk a lot when they're nervous. I'm not talking. I don't want to talk to anybody. I think I'm getting a little bit nervous.

We walk out of the hall onto the range. The archery range is huge and super bright. The wood floors look like a basketball court with bright ceiling lights. At the far end were giant blocks of foam against the wall, as tall as an adult. That's where we will shoot. They are eighteen meters away. I know because I read the rules. That is how far away I've been practicing. On the archer end, there are so many people, all different kinds, with all different kinds of bows. And, not a single pink one. I look at my bow and then at everyone else's. Mine is tiny, but it's mine and I like it a whole bunch.

Behind the shooting line, there are stands for your bow. I put mine with the others behind lane A-1. That's my shooting lane, all the way at the end against the wall.

The bow stand is too wide for my small bow. I think I have the smallest bow and I think I am the smallest archer, all by myself at the end.

I put my bow on the ground and lean it on my bow stand. I lean out past the shooting line and look down the range at the other archers. Most were adults. There are some kids, but they all look like teenagers.

I must be the youngest kid here. I can tell because whenever people walk past me, they stop to watch or slow down and smile. It's weird. They point at my bow. Some whisper. Others wink.

I just stand there. I get out my quiver and put in my arrows. I'm an archer, I tell myself. Dad asks me if everything is OK for like the twentieth time.

"I'm fine, Dad."

I see Riley on her iPad sitting next to Mom, against the wall behind all of us archers.

I continue arranging my arrows. They all look the same: long and black with white and pink feathers. But, I have my favorite ones, the ones that always hit the X. They go in the front of my quiver. Then, I have my second favorites. Those go next. The back of my quiver is empty. That's the "Naughty Corner." When I shoot, if my arrow doesn't go where I want, it goes in the Naughty Corner for a time out. I don't like to use an arrow that's in the Naughty Corner.

"Archers!" The judge in the red shirt yells out. There are about five of them all over the range.

"Place your target at the end of your lane. We will start the warm up ends in two minutes."

I bet Dad reminds me it will start in. . . .

"Addy, two minutes." Really Dad?!

Chapter 13: The Zoo

Dad keeps telling me to relax. I take a big deep breath so he can see I'm relaxing. I think he needs to relax. He has a nervous look in his eyes. Dad keeps looking over to Mom and back at me. I mean really, do I look funny or something? I'm sure I don't. I always dress myself and I always look good. I've said it before and it's still true, I have an eye for fashion.

Dad finally takes a deep breath himself. I stand in front of him. He looks down at me with his hands on my shoulders. He always has so much to say. Like way too much. But, he just stares at me. I look up at him trying to make him feel better.

"I'm fine, Dad." Dad's big hands are still on my shoulders.

"Are you sure you have everything? Drink some more water. Ignore the other kids." Blah, blah, blah. "OK, Addy have fun!"

I wish he would stop worrying. It's not like it's the Olympics or something. I'm trying to have fun, if he'd let me. I know what I'm doing. All the archers walk to the shooting line and start walking down the lanes with their targets. I have mine, my first real target. It's just a piece of big paper, but it's so cool. My nail polish matches all the colors on the target—black, blue, red, yellow, and the spider! I painted a special black X on each of my middle fingers, because, that is what I wanted.

I walk slower than everyone else, with my target, so I can see what they do. I'm not sure where to put it on the foam bail. In the rules, Dad can't come down the lane. He can't even come to the shooting line. He has to stay behind another line behind the shooting line. They even say he can't talk to me or anything until I come back behind the line with him.

So, I watch the other archers put up their targets. I remember we have to put them in a special place for our lane, but I can't remember where. I need to figure this out. Everyone is going to be done soon and I will be the only one left out here.

I notice another girl walking down the range toward me. She must be late. I see behind her, back at the line, a man who must be her Dad. He is waving some kind of directions to her. She keeps walking toward me.

She looks older than me, maybe eleven or twelve like my sister, Riley. She has blond hair in a ponytail like me, but she has a hat on and a blue shirt. She's wearing pants, not a skirt like me. I can help her look more fashionable, but I like her white hat; a good choice.

She walks up next to me. We look at each other and don't say anything. We have other things on our minds, like where to hang our target before we are totally embarrassed!

Finally, a judge walks over to us. He looks like Santa Claus in his red shirt and white beard.

"You ladies need help with your target placement?"

Girls! Sheesh!

We nod. I don't think we are ready to talk to Santa Claus.

"Ok. This is how it works. You're in line A . . . blah, blah . . . upper left . . . blah, blah . .

. your line B . . . blah, blah . . . take turns . . . blah, blah . . . shoot the right target. Got it?"

What the heck! The girl and I both glance at each other, then back at Santa. We both nod yes, but knew we had no idea what he just said.

I'm just going to shoot the target she isn't going to shoot.

Santa smiles at us. We stare at him. He has a funny look on his face.

"OK, ladies. Good luck!"

That's when I look around. Oh no! We are the only ones at the target end of the range. The whole place is looking at us! We start fast walking back to the shooting line. I'm going so fast, I hold my hand on my quiver so it won't bounce around clanging my arrows and drawing more attention to us. Right when we get to the line a buzzer goes off and scares me so much I jump.

"This begins the two warm up rounds. After that we will start scoring."

Beeeeeeep! I jump again. The warm up clock starts ticking down.

Finally, I can walk to the shooting line and get this started. I just love shooting my bow and that is all I want to do. Time to warm up.

I'm so glad parents have to stay behind us. The parent line is funny. They can't come near us, they can't talk to us. They just lean as far as they can over the line making funny faces. It looks like they're in pain.

I shoot a warm up arrow on my super awesome bow. I can't stop looking back at the parent line. They look like zoo animals trying to

escape out of their cages. Everyone except Riley.
I bet she doesn't even know we started shooting.

I shoot some more warm up arrows.
Awesome! An X. I hit the center of the target. I
look back at Dad. He winks at me. Mom smiles.
I like that. It's better than talking. Sometimes I
don't think Dad knows what he is saying. At
practice he tells me to focus. Focus on my form.
Block everything out of my mind and a bunch
of other stuff. Then, he's always talking behind
me while I shoot.

"OK, Addy. Do you understand what I'm
saying?" I have no idea what he's talking about.

"Were you listening to what I was
saying?" No. I was shooting. I was blocking you
out. You told me to focus. See, he doesn't make
any sense.

I look at my Dad behind the zoo cage with the other crazy parents. I smile at him. He likes that. He smiles back. I smile at him all the time, even when things aren't going well. It'll help him make it through the tournament and he'll stop giving me so much advice. Dad crosses his arm with a proud look watching me warm up.

I shoot some more warm up arrows. The warm up clock is counting down to the start. I don't even have to look at the clock. You can just look at the parents and tell the scoring rounds are about to start. They're getting more fidgety, whispering with each other, squirming around and drinking their coffees real fast. Yep, the scoring will start soon.

I will never understand them. They all pester us and as soon as the scoring clock starts, and when we shoot the first arrow, they all look away! Some parents try to look out of the corner of their eye. Some peek through their fingers. One mom looks real quick to see where the arrow hits and then looks away real fast. I don't get it. Weird.

I used to close my eyes when I shot my arrow and then open them to see where it went. Maybe parents are afraid of where the arrow will go? The first time I shot a bow I didn't know what it would do.

Chapter 14: Oh No!!

I look back at Dad. He smiles as best he can through a worried looking face. I don't smile and look back at my target.

I take a deep breath and wait for the starting buzzer. There it is: my target, eighteen meters away. That's fifty-nine feet, a long way. It sure looks far away right now. A lot farther away than it did in practice. I stare at it. The target just sits there staring back at me from the big foam bail. It has wood all around the edges holding the bail on the wall. The lights are bright.

It is quiet, really quiet now.

Beeeeeep! - THWAK! THWAK-THWAK-THWAK-THWAK-THWAK!

I jump again and I look down the line real fast. Everyone is shooting. Like a hundred people. Giant bows in the air shooting arrows into the targets. Some bows as big as me! They make a real loud sound.

THWAK!

I look up at the two minute timer. We only have two minutes to shoot this end.

THWAK-THWAK.

I look back at my target. I look down at my arrows. I pull an arrow from one of my favorite. I put it on my bow and nock it on the string. I feel like I'm in slow motion.

I raise my bow and arrow, the target stares back at me. I draw back, find my anchor at the corner of my mouth. I aim with my scope, the target comes into focus. This is it.

Everything is quiet again . . . and I shoot.

THWAK!

I look down the range. I hit it! I hit the
target! OK it isn't the greatest shot and this is
only warm up, but I'm happy I don't hit the
floor or the ceiling, or the wrong target. I hit it!

I look back at Dad and he has a big smile
and winks at me. I smile back quickly and look
away. I'm happy he's there but embarrassed he's
smiling at me.

We shoot another end of arrows for
warm up and now the scoring starts. So far, I hit
the target or the foam bail every time.
Everything is going well.

The warm up timer at the Championships
is finished. The parents behind the zoo line get
quiet. We are going to shoot our first scoring

arrows. I'm focused on what I've been practicing. A long time. In the freezing rain.

Today, we were going to shoot 60 arrows for scoring. I shot a lot of arrows since I first tried Grandpa's bow. I was really here.

"This is the first scoring end!" The judge yells across the range. The whistle blows and the two minute timer starts counting down.
I draw my first arrow to score, and shoot.

CRACK!

I jump and my eyes get big. What was that?! It sounded like someone threw a rock at a wall. I look down the range at my target. I look at the shooting line. A lot of people were looking down the range at me. What are they looking at?

Uh oh! I slowly look back at my target. There isn't an arrow anywhere on it. I look around. Oops! There it is stuck in the wood between the targets. Oh darn it, my first arrow. I still have a minute left and have to shoot two more arrows.

OK, Addy, I tell myself. Just forget about it. It's only one arrow. There are a lot left to go.

Don't look at anyone. Who cares if they stare at you? Just look at the target.

I draw my second arrow and shoot. Thwak! Thwak! Thwak! The first arrows hit the target. That sounded better. But it's in the foam, not the target. The zoo parents start taking pictures of us with their iPhones. I think it's funny they take so many pictures of something they don't want to look at.

I draw my third arrow. I aim right on the X.

Crack!

Oh man, not again. Even Riley looks up and Mom looks at Dad like he should do something. I don't even look down the line. I know they're all looking at me, thinking, who's the kid, what's she doing here, is she ready for this tournament?

I'm getting a little nervous and look back at Dad. He always believes in me. He'll tell me it's OK, that everything will be fine. Dad is waving me over to him with a panicked look on his face.

Great. The one person, at this crucial moment of my life that I need support from, looks like he is watching a disaster. Couldn't he just pretend everything is fine?

I want to walk over to him but the whistle blows for us to remove our arrows. I walk slightly backwards, look at Dad then turn away towards the target. Dad stands there, he looks alarmed.

The end is over. I take the long walk down the range to pull my arrows out of the wood. I wiggle my stuck arrows to get them out. Other archers look over at me, concerned. I

don't look at them. I don't need help. I can do
this myself.

Walking back to the line seems to take
forever. The second wave of archers, the
shooting partners, wait on the line. There must
be a hundred of them. Everyone is serious,
focused. Everyone must feel like I do. I narrow
my eyes. Well, not quite. They didn't just put
their arrows in the wood.

Looking down my lane, I see the girl in
the white hat. I walk closer, my arrows clanking
in the quiver around my waist. As I pass behind
the line, we look at each other. We are trying to
figure out if we are friends or frenemies. That's
what girls do. First, we decide you are wearing
cool clothes. That helps us decide if we will talk.
Then we stare at each other, decide if we need a
new friend and if you mix with our other
friends. Then, are you competition? Do I want

to be friends with a girl I want to beat? It's kind of weird and really complicated, but it's just the way it is. Mom says it never changes.

I think I'll try and change it. I smile at her. Her face get's a concerned look. She doesn't smile back. See, she didn't see that coming. I think I'll make her my friend.

I walk back to Dad while the other girl, my shooting partner, my new friend, begins shooting.

"What's wrong? What happened? Are you OK?"

"I'm OK Dad, but my arrows are flying everywhere. Something's wrong."

"Well, let me take a look at your bow."

It was nice he was going to take a look, but he doesn't know anything about bows. I'm not even sure what he is going to look at. Last time he did this he was holding it upside down.

"Look Addy! Your scope is broken!"

Wow. Dad sees the problem right away. Dads are kind of impressive that way. They can fix lots of things that they don't even know about. I was glad Mom had Dad doing lots of practice fixing things around the house every weekend. It's probably why he can see how to fix my scope.

"I don't think I can fix it Addy. But, that's why you can't aim."

Oh, great. I'm going to be hitting the wood all day. This is the worst. My first tournament and it's already a disaster. What am I going to do?

I look at Dad, fighting back tears. I'm not going to cry. I'm not going to cry. I can't quit now. I keep thinking: I have to finish. I have to finish. I am an archer!

"Dad, can we put my old one back on?" I remember that we had an old one I haven't used much. It isn't really a scope, just a little pin that sticks out. But at least I can aim with it, I hope.

"Good idea Addy! Do you think you can shoot with it?" I just shrug.

"I have to Dad."

Dad gets a big grin on his face and gives me a giant hug. He doesn't say anything and just starts going to work real fast on my bow. It's the best when they don't say anything. Parents always ruin a good hug with lots of blabbing and then they kiss you.

Dad's hug makes me feel better. I think he's saying that he's proud of me. He better be. This wasn't easy, standing here with a broken bow and two more days of shooting to go.

Inside, I want to cry and leave, but a little bit of me wants to prove I'm an archer. I just focus on that little bit. I think that is the bit that Dad hugged.

Chapter 15: Back On the Line

There are only thirty seconds left and
Dad is still screwing in the pin sight. Hurry,
hurry. The clock is counting down, twenty,
nineteen, eighteen. . . . Hurry, Dad!

"I think this is it Addy." Dad hands me
the bow.

I walk back to the shooting line, five,
four, three . . . I look down at my necklace. It's a
multi-colored target, just like the one I'm
shooting. Mom and Dad had given it to me a
few days before the tournament.

They took me out for hot chocolate at
Starbucks, without my sister so I knew

something was up. They got their usual coffees.
Well, Mom always gets a double non-fat latte
with an Equal, Dad, he just gets black coffee
with nothing. So gross. I tasted it once and spit
it out in the garbage. Everything Dad drinks and
eats is gross, but he always makes us try a bite.
"Try it once, and then you can say you don't like
it," he says. My sister and I try to find stuff Dad
won't eat, but we haven't come up with anything
yet. I always get hot chocolate.

When we got there, we walked right past
the wooden chairs and tables and Dad sunk into
one of the big couches. This was a good sign.
Whatever they were going to talk about wasn't
very serious. I relaxed.

Mom took out a small box and gave it to
me. In it was the necklace I'm wearing now.

"So you will always keep your dreams on target," Mom said. I gave her a big hug.

Today, on the line, I reach up and hold the target necklace in my hand and rub it. I'm going to finish this.

Beeeeep! The shooting clock starts. Two minutes. THWAK! I hit the outside of the target. I take a deep breath. Not a good shot, but at least not wood. My next two shots hit in the same area. Looks like I'll have to adjust my sight, but at least I'll be on the target.

I look back at Dad. His arms are folded with a concerned look. I smile at him. It's going to be fine Dad.

I can see him relax a little. I'm relaxed. Here we go.

By the end of the day, I had shot sixty arrows while standing at the line for three hours. I don't think I did very well but most of my arrows are on the target. I'm tired.

I still have the second round tomorrow. I wonder if I should wear the same outfit both days?

Chapter 16: A New Friend

We arrive early the next day. I walk in and set up my bow and start stretching. Yeah, I'm the smallest one here, but I'm one of them.

The white hat girl that was shooting in my lane is back again. We decide to talk.

"Hi," I smiled.

"Hi."

She seems nice. She sees me stretching and starts stretching with me.

"I'm Addy. This, is my first tournament."

"I'm Karissa."

Not much. She must still be deciding on me. Maybe I'll try again. She has on a cool archery shirt. She looks like she's from a team.

"Are you on an Archery Team?"

"Yes." OK, maybe she's just quiet.

"I just learned to do archery. How long have you been doing archery? I like your shirt. It's cool."

"Thanks." Then she turned her head down fast and took a step to the line.

I look back. There behind the coaching line is the big guy again, waving and making hand gestures at Karissa. He's trying to say something.

"Is that your Dad?" I roll my eyes.

"I have one too. They just embarrass you all the time don't they?"

She picks up her bow and smiles at me. "They just don't stop." She glances back at her dad.

"All the time they are trying to help," she goes on, "to give advice, asking questions over and over again. I'm so glad they have the line back there."

I stare at my target. "Ugh! Me too."

"My Dad helps sometimes, but most of the time he just says the same stuff over and over again."

Karissa looks up at her target. "They're kind of funny looking back there. They look like trapped octopuses who can't talk, waving their hands all around."

I moved my hand to my quiver ready to pull an arrow.   "Totally!"

Beeeep!

I think I made a friend!

Karissa and I shoot together the rest of the day. She's older and better than me, but it's fun to shoot with another girl about my age. We talk and keep score together. I watch her shoot and try to copy what she's doing. Karissa says she's on the Select Archery Team. That's why she has the cool shirt with her name on it. Someday I'll be on an archery team. I just have to keep practicing. We finish up day two of the National tournament and turn in our score cards.

It's done! I did it! I finished the whole tournament.

"How do you think you did Addy." Dad walks up to me with a smile.

"I did real good. I think I might be way up in the top girls. And, it was real fun. I made a friend."

Dad crouches down in front of me.

"Addy, I am real proud of how well you did, but let's not get our hopes up too high. I don't think you're going to get a medal and if you aren't ranked very high, it's OK. This was your first tournament. Just practice. Does that make sense?"

Really? Can't I just enjoy it for a minute? Parents are all about "reality" and "don't get your hopes up." Why not? Why can't I get my hopes up?

That's why I did the tournament in the first place, because my hopes were up. If I just thought about "reality" all day, about all the stuff I have to do, like chores and homework, then I'd be doing the same thing over and over again every day and never do anything fun. That would be horrible. If you did that you would never smile.

"Dad! I think I did really good."

Dad looks me in the eyes. Uh oh, he really wants me to listen now.

"Addy, you did. You really did. But I just want you to understand that it might not be as good as you think. I don't want you to be let down."

"I won't be let down Dad." I spin around to pack away my bow and turn my head back at him smiling.

"I probably took first."

He looks up at the ceiling and then down at me. Maybe he's looking for how high my hopes are.

The results are going to come out in two weeks. They have to add up the scores of all the girls in the whole country, even me.

Chapter 17: Results

I watch the National Championships
website every day for two weeks. I wait and wait
to see the scores. Maybe tomorrow.

The next day, I log on to my sister's
laptop at breakfast, before school. When the
website comes up, there it is. FINALLY! The
results of the National Tournament!

"Dad! Dad! The results!"

I run to the bathroom where Dad is
shaving.

"The results!"

I stand in the doorway with my hands on
my hips. He looks startled and then a smile

opens on his shaving cream face, but not too much of a smile because Dad doesn't get excited about anything.

"So, how did you do?" He asks without being excited.

"I don't know. I didn't look."
My mouth drops open and my eyes get big. I was so excited, I forgot to look. I spin around and run back through the house to look.

"I know! I know how I did!" I come running back up to Dad and his shaving. This time Mom and even Riley come up behind me to see what all the fuss was about.

"Tell me."

"No. You guess!"

I grin real big. I'm not going to tell him. He doesn't have his hopes up and I know he will guess wrong.

"Well, there have to be a lot of girls in your age bracket around the country. You shot well, but this is just your first tournament." He squints his eyes to think about it.

"I'm guessing you were somewhere between sixtieth and fiftieth place?"

"NOPE!" I put my hands back on my hips.

"Come on Addy! Tell us." Even my sister wanted to know.

"Nineteenth!! I'm Nineteenth!!" I stare squarely at Dad.

"Nineteenth? WOW!" Dad puts down his razor and leans on the counter. "I can't believe it." He actually looked excited!!

Mom hugs me from behind.

"I did it! I'm an archer! I'm an archer!"

I run through the house announcing it to my Mom and sister.

"That's awesome Addy." Riley yelled from her room. She was really excited, for a minute.

I gave Mom a big hug, "Congratulations sweetheart!"

I run back to Dad and gave him a hug. Then, I do another lap around the house yelling. This is the best!

In the tournament, it had been really hard watching my arrows hit the wood, then my scope broke. It had been hard to get my parents to even let me go to the tournament. When I'd finally walked in I didn't even look like I belonged. I was the youngest and smallest and everyone thought my bow was a toy.

But, I really wanted to be an archer. I didn't care what anyone thought or what happened. I just knew if I kept shooting my arrows eventually I would be as good as everyone else.

What an awesome day!

I had never heard of archery when Grandpa showed us the bow. I wasn't even sure I wanted to do archery. I thought it was for boys. I'm glad I wasn't afraid to try something new because it's turned out real fun. And, my parents have learned to relax . . . a little.

Take Aim ...

...Titles and...

Book 1: I'm Trying Something New!

Coming Soon....

Book 2: Balance and Responsibility.

Book 3: New Friends and Competition.

… at Future

…Social Media!

Book 4: Everything is Right! Then All Wrong.

Book 5: You Have to Have Fun.

And many more books to come!

www.ArcherAddy.com

About Archer Addy

Addison Nachtrieb is a competitive target archer who lives in Seattle, WA. She currently shoots a Compound Bow Freestyle. Addy has been practicing archery since September 2012 and competing since February 2013. She has just begun her archery journey and is having fun learning, practicing, and competing. Besides learning archery skills, Addy has learned how to be dedicated and focused on achieving a goal. She has seen success. She lives with her family in West Seattle and is now eleven and in the 5th grade. Stories in the Archer Addy book series are based on true events, and most are taken from Addy's archery journal, where she records her experiences.

Addy shoots out of Next Step Archery on the select archery team and shoots for Team

Nock Point in Washington State. She is currently the, **2014 - NFAA 3-D National Champion, Redding CA. Score (1524/1540).**

About the Authors

Erik and Tracy Nachtrieb have now added published authors to their list of creative projects all derived from their work in television, film and video. As producers of adventure content, they know how to identify a unique story and bring it to life. In addition, Erik is an adventure/expedition cameraman having worked on a wide range of projects. As new archery parents, they look forward to bringing the story of archery and determination to a blossoming generation. They hope young children enjoy this series and find inspiration to try something new and to challenge themselves.

About the Illustrator

In the *Archer Addy* theme of "inspired youth," at seventeen years old, Hayden Beaty is the illustrator for the first book in the *Archer Addy* series. Hayden became interested in drawing when he was eleven. Since that time, he has developed many artistic styles and applies a broad range of techniques to his work. This passion and talent lead Hayden to illustrate *Archer Addy,* his first book. Hayden holds the highest rank of Eagle Scout, in the Boy Scouts of America, studies martial arts and, speaks Japanese as a second language. Recently, he has also learned a great deal about archery.

Made in the
USA
Middletown, DE